FUN JOKES!

FOR FUNNY KIDS

Reader's
Digest

New York / Montreal

Table of Contents

A Note from the Editors

Reader's Digest is the world's #1 collector of humor—for everyone from age 6 to 106. In *Fun Jokes for Funny Kids, Volume 2*, we've compiled the best of the best for our youngest readers. We asked one witty girl to tell us which ones she liked most; you'll see Alexa's Favorites sprinkled throughout the book.

Now we're inviting parents of budding comedians to send jokes for our next volume. Submit your child's riddles, one-liners, puns, and more at **rd.com/jokesforkids**.

About Alexa

Alexa is a third-grader who lives in New York City. She still loves gymnastics, tacos, and the color pink.

Knock!
Knock!

Who's there . . . ?

7

A Shoe-morous Joke

Knock! Knock!

Who's there?

Wooden shoe.

Wooden shoe who?

Wooden shoe like to hear another joke?

Snow

Knock! Knock!

Who's there?

Snow.

Snow who?

Snow use. I forgot my name again!

Honeydew

Knock! Knock!

Who's there?

Honeydew.

Honeydew who?

Honeydew you want to hear some garden jokes?

---------- ★ **ALEXA'S FAVORITE**

Wendy

Knock! Knock!
　Who's there?
Wendy.
　Wendy who?

Wendy bell works again I won't have to knock anymore.

- -

Tired

Knock! Knock!
Gary.
　Gary who?
Gary me, I'm too tired to go any further.

Water

Knock! Knock!
　Who's there?
Water.
　Water who?
Water those plants or they're going to die!

Boo Hoo

Knock! Knock!
  Who's there?
Boo hoo.
  Boo hoo who?
Aww, don't cry—it's just a joke.

Carmen

Knock! Knock!
  Who's there?
Carmen.
  Carmen who?
Carmen let me in already!

Needle

Knock! Knock!
  Who's there?
Needle.
  Needle who?
Needle little help gettin' in the door.

Ida

Knock! Knock!
   Who's there?
Ida.
   Ida who?
Idaho the garden.

Doughnut

Knock! Knock!
   Who's there?
Doughnut.
   Doughnut who?
Doughnut leave me out there.

Voodoo

Knock! Knock!
   Who's there?
Voodoo.
   Voodoo who?
Voodoo you think you are asking me so many questions?

Says

Knock! Knock!
   Who's there?
Says.
   Says who?
Says me, that's who!

- - - - - - - - - - ★ **ALEXA'S FAVORITE**

Justin

Knock! Knock!
   Who's there?
Justin.
   Justin who?

Justin the neighborhood and thought I'd come over.

- -

Under the Weather

Knock! Knock!
   Who's there?
H.
   H who?
Bless you!

Pecan

Knock! Knock!
   Who's there?
Pecan.
   Pecan who?
Pecan somebody your own size!

Candice

Knock! Knock!
   Who's there?
Candice.
   Candice who?
Candice door open, or what?

Godiva

Knock! Knock!
   Who's there?
Godiva.
   Godiva who?
Godiva terrible headache. Do you have an aspirin?

Harry

Knock! Knock!
   Who's there?
Harry.
   Harry who?
Harry up and let me in!

Amarillo Man

Knock! Knock!
   Who's there?
Amarillo.
   Amarillo who?
Amarillo nice guy!

Robin

Knock! Knock!
   Who's there?
Robin.
   Robin who?
Robin you! Hand over your cash!

Claire

Knock! Knock!

Who's there?

Claire.

Claire who?

Claire the way; I'm coming in!

Ken

Knock! Knock!

Who's there?

Ken.

Ken who?

Ken you let me in?

T-Rex

Knock! Knock!

Who's there?

T-Rex.

T-Rex who?

There is a T-Rex at your door and you want to know his name!?!

Santa

Knock! Knock!
  Who's there?
Santa.
  Santa who?
Santa email reminding you I'd be here, and you STILL make me wait in the cold!

Interrupting Cow

Knock! Knock!
  Who's there?
Interrupting cow.
  Interruptin-
Mooooo!

Hanna

Knock! Knock!
  Who's there?
Hanna.
  Hanna who?
Hanna partridge in a pear tree!

Banana

Knock! Knock!
   Who's there?
Banana
   Banana who?
Banana split, so ice creamed.

Will

Knock! Knock!
   Who's there?
Will.
   Will who?
Will you just open the door already?

---------- ★ **ALEXA'S FAVORITE**

Dozen

Knock! Knock!
   Who's there?
Dozen.
   Dozen who?
Dozen anyone want to let me in?

- -

Avenue

Knock! Knock!
  Who's there?
Avenue.
  Avenue who?
Avenue knocked on this door before?

- - - - - - - - - - ★ **ALEXA'S FAVORITE**

Witches

Knock! Knock!
  Who's there?
Witches.
  Witches who?
Witches the way home?

- -

To Whom It May Concern

Knock! Knock!
  Who's there?
To.
  To who?
No, to whom.

Check

Knock! Knock!
　Who's there?
Check.
　Check who?
Check first before you open the door.

Wanda

Knock! Knock!
　Who's there?
Wanda.
　Wanda who?
Wanda hang out with me right now?

Yule Log

Knock! Knock!
　Who's there?
Yule log.
　Yule log who?
Yule log the door after you let me in, won't you?

Quirky
Q&A's

A Flower

Q: Why is the letter A like a flower?

A: Because a bee comes after it.

Raining Money

Q: When does it rain money?

A: When there is a "change" in the weather.

Evaporating Raindrop

Q: What did the evaporating raindrop say?

A: I'm going to pieces.

Toto, We're Not In Kansas Anymore...

Q: What did the Tin Man say when he got run over by a steamroller?

A: "Curses! Foiled again!"

Discount Shopping

Q: Where does a one-armed man shop?

A: At a secondhand store.

- - - - - - - - - - ★ **ALEXA'S FAVORITE**

Sprinkling Rain

Q: What does it do before it rains candy?

A: It sprinkles!

- -

Ocean Waving

Q: What did the ocean say to the sailboat?

A: Nothing, it just waved.

Cloud Undies

Q: What kind of shorts do clouds wear?

A: Thunderwear

Horses and Weather

Q: What's the difference between a horse and the weather?

A: One is reined up and the other rains down.

Avocado James

Q: What's an avocado's favorite music?

A: Guac 'n' roll.

Dracula's Dog

Q: What kind of dog does Dracula have?

A: A bloodhound!

Sick Banana

Q: Why did the banana go to the doctor?

A: It wasn't peeling well.

Extra Purrr-estrial

Q: What did the alien say to the cat?

A: "Take me to your litter."

Bottoms Up

Q: What sits at the bottom of the ocean and twitches?

A: A nervous wreck.

Parking Lot Dog

Q: Why did the dog cross the road?

A: To get to the barking lot!

It's a Phase

Q: How does the Man in the Moon cut his hair?

A: Eclipse it!

Funny Mutt

Q: What breed of dog tells off-color jokes?

A: A smutt.

- - - - - - - - - - ★ **ALEXA'S FAVORITE**

Grapes Make Wine

Q: What did the grape do when he got stepped on?

A: He let out a little wine.

- -

Mexico Weather

Q: What is the Mexican weather report?

A: Chili today and hot tamale.

Rise and Shine

Q: What do cats like to eat for breakfast?

A: Mice Krispies.

Old VWs

Q: Where do Volkswagens go when they get old?

A: The old Volks home.

Plant Pals

Q: What did the big flower say to the little flower?

A: Hi, bud!

Music-to-Go

Q: Why do bagpipe players walk while they play?

A: To get away from the noise.

Fizz for Felines

Q: Which two sodas does a cat like best?

A: Dr. Peppurr and Meowntain Mew.

Snowman's Savings

Q: Where do snowmen keep their money?

A: In a snowbank.

Poor Kitty

Q: What did the cat say when he went bankrupt?

A: I feel so paw!

All Up in Your Grill

Q: What do you call a grilled cheese sandwich that gets right up in your face?

A: Too-close-for-comfort food.

Rapper Rain

Q: Why does Snoop Dog need an umbrella?

A: Fo' Drizzle.

Fashionista Kitty

Q: Why did the cat wear a dress?

A: She was feline fine.

Duck Movie

Q: What type of movie is about water fowl?

A: A duckumentary.

- - - - - - - - - - ★ ALEXA'S FAVORITE

Air

Q: What is the thing that you and I are always crashing in to?

A: Air, silly!!

- -

Tee up the Band

Q: What's a golf club's favorite type of music?

A: Swing.

--------- ★ **ALEXA'S FAVORITE**

Hand in Hand

Q: What did the finger say to the thumb?

A: I'm in glove with you!

The Lying Snowman

Q: What do you call a snowman that tells tall tales?

A: A snow-fake!

Sugar-Free

Q: What do you call someone who can't stick with a diet?

A: A desserter.

Sweet Romance

Q: Why did the apricot ask a prune to dinner?

A: Because he couldn't find a date.

A Love of Biblical Proportions

Q: Did Adam and Eve ever have a date?

A: No, they had an apple!

The Music Thieves

Q: Why did the burglars decide to rob a music store?

A: For the lute.

Two Ships Passing in the Night

Q: What did the little boat say to the yacht?

A: Can I interest you in a little row-mance?

- - - - - - - - - - ★ **ALEXA'S FAVORITE**

Changing of Seasons

Q: Can February March?

A: No, but April May.

- -

Ridiculous
Riddles

Share Me

Q: If you have me, you want to share me.
If you share me, you haven't got me.
What am I?

A: A secret.

Poor People Have It...

Q: Poor people have it. Rich people need it.
If you eat it, you'll die. What is it?

A: Nothing!

100 Feet

Q: It's 100 feet in the air, yet its back is on
the ground. What is it?

A: A centipede on its back.

Always Getting Older

Q: What goes up and never comes down?

A: Your age!

What Kind of Coat...

Q: What kind of coat is always wet when you put it on?

A: A coat of paint.

Thinking Pink

Q: There's a one-story house where everything inside is pink: pink walls, pink doors, pink floors, pink ceilings, pink windows, pink curtains, pink chairs, and pink tables. What color are the stairs?

A: There are none—it's a one-story house!

- - - - - - - - - - ★ ALEXA'S FAVORITE

An Enlightening Riddle

Q: I weigh nothing, but you can still see me. If you put me in a bucket, I make the bucket lighter. What am I?

A: A hole!

- -

Butcher

Q: Paul's height is 6 feet, he's an assistant at a butcher's shop, and wears size 9 shoes. What does he weigh?

A: Meat.

Crabby!

Q: What do you get if you cross an apple with a shellfish?

A: A crab apple!

Watercolor

Q: What goes in the water black and comes out red?

A: A lobster.

Ouch!

Q: What is black, white, and red all over?

A: A sunburned penguin!

Copycats

Q: There were 10 cats in a boat and one jumped out. How many were left?

A: None, because they were all a bunch of copycats.

What Has 13 Hearts...

Q: What has 13 hearts, but no other organs?

A: A deck of playing cards.

Finish the Sequence

Q: Name the next letter in this sequence: J F M A M J J A S O N ?

A: D. The sequence contains the first letter of every month, in order.

Imposter

Q: What do you call a fake noodle?

A: An Impasta.

- - - - - - - - - - ★ **ALEXA'S FAVORITE**

Cracking Up

Q: Why did Humpty Dumpty have a great fall?

A: To make up for his miserable summer.

- -

Dog and Bee

Q: What do you get when you cross a race dog with a bumblebee?

A: A Greyhound buzz.

Cowbells

Q: Why do cows have bells?

A: Because their horns don't work.

3 Feet

Q: What has 3 feet but cannot walk?

A: A yardstick.

How Far Can a Fox...

Q: How far can a fox run into a grove?

A: Only halfway—then he's running out of it!

A Man Rode In...

Q: A man rode in to town on Tuesday and left two days later on Tuesday. How so?

A: His horse is named Tuesday!

Pickle Pun

Q: What did one pickle say to the other pickle who wouldn't stop complaining?

A: "Dill with it."

Write On

Q: What's a writing utensil's favorite place to go on vacation?

A: Pencil-vania!

A Lot to Think About

Q: I have hundreds of wheels, but move,
I do not. Call me what I am: Call me a lot.
What am I?

A: A parking lot.

What's The Different Between A Cat...

Q: What's the different between a cat and
a comma?

A: A cat has claws at the end of paws;
a comma is a pause at the end of a
clause.

The Man Who Made It...

Q: The man who made it doesn't want it.
The man who bought it doesn't need it.
The man who needs it doesn't know it.
What am I talking about?

A: A coffin.

Window-Washing

Q: A man is washing windows on the 25th floor of an apartment building. Suddenly, he slips and falls. He has nothing to cushion his fall and no safety equipment—but he doesn't get hurt. How is this possible?

A: He's washing windows inside the building.

Jeweler vs. Jailer

Q: What's the difference between a jeweler and a prison guard?

A: A jeweler sells watches, and a prison guard watches cells!

Answer Me!

Q: You answer me, but I never ask you a question. What am I?

A: The telephone.

Not

Q: Forward I am heavy, but backward I am not. What am I?

A: Forward I am ton, backward I am not.

Yellow Bus

Q: What is big and yellow and comes in the morning to brighten Mom's day?

A: The school bus.

Brother!

Q: You are my brother, but I am not your brother. Who am I?

A: Your sister.

What Word Begins...

Q: What word begins and ends with an E but only has one letter?

A: Envelope!

With Pointed Fangs I...

Q: With pointed fangs I sit and wait; with piercing force I crunch out fate; grabbing victims, proclaiming might; physically joining with a single bite. What am I?

A: A stapler.

- - - - - - - - - - ★ ALEXA'S FAVORITE

Pedestrian Crossing

Q: A man was driving a truck. His headlights weren't on, and the moon wasn't out. Ahead of him, a woman dressed in all black started crossing the road. Fortunately, the man braked so she could cross. How did he see her?

A: It was the middle of the day!

- -

Stories

Q: What building has the most stories?

A: A library.

Hold Me

Q: I am light as a feather, yet the strongest man can't hold me for more than 5 minutes. What am I?

A: A breath.

Cracked, Made, Told

Q: I can be cracked, I can be made, I can be told, I can be played. What am I?

A: A joke.

Oh, Onion!

Q: You use a knife to slice my head and weep beside me when I'm dead. What am I?

A: An onion.

Eye

Q: What has a single eye but cannot see?

A: A needle.

Anchors Away

Q: When you need me, you throw me away. But when you're done with me, you bring me back. What am I?

A: An anchor.

Why Is Six Afraid...

Q: Why is the number six afraid of seven?

A: Because seven ate nine!

Brown or Silver

Q: What is brown or silver, has a head and tail but no arms or legs?

A: A coin.

No Movement

Q: What goes up and down the stairs without moving?

A: Carpet.

Raining

Q: No matter how much rain comes down on it, it won't get any wetter. What is it?

A: Water.

---------- ★ **ALEXA'S FAVORITE**

Horse Sense

Q: A horse attached to a 24-foot chain sees an apple 26 feet away. How can the horse reach the apple?

A: The horse just walks over to it, taking the chain with him—the chain isn't attached to anything!

Why Are Football Stadiums...

Q: Why are football stadiums so cool?

A: Because every seat has a fan in it!

Heads Up

Q: What loses its head in the morning and gets it back at night?

A: A pillow.

Cowboy Hats

Q: Why are cowboy hats turned up on the sides?

A: So that three people can fit in the pickup.

Which Dinosaur Knew...

Q: Which dinosaur knew the most words?

A: The thesaurus.

Dry Drowning

Q: When will a man drown but not get wet?

A: When he's trapped in quicksand.

One-Liners

Snack Attack

• • •

If we're not meant to have midnight snacks,
why is there a light in the fridge?

Born to be Negative

• • •

I was born to be a pessimist.
My blood type is B negative.

Campfire

• • •

How is it one careless match can start
a forest fire, but it takes a whole box
to start a campfire?

Fitness Tip

• • •

The trouble with jogging is that by the
time you realize you're not in shape for it,
it's too far to walk back.

Welcome to the World
• • •

When I was born, I was so surprised,
I didn't talk for a year and a half.

- - - - - - - - - - ★ **ALEXA'S FAVORITE**

Construction Work Ahead
• • •

Want to hear a joke about construction?
I'm still working on it.

- -

Shut Down Haters
• • •

Hippo 1: You're fat.
Hippo 2: That's very hippo-critical.

Plunge
• • •

Never test the depth of the water
with both feet.

Supercharged Swine

• • •

A pig stands in front of an electric socket:
"Oh no, who put you into that wall?!"

Don't Have a Bird

• • •

My boyfriend told me to stop acting like a
flamingo. So I had to put my foot down.

Early Bird

• • •

The early bird might get the worm, but the
second mouse gets the cheese

---------- ★ ALEXA'S FAVORITE

Clones

• • •

Clones are people two!

How Does This Joke Stack Up?
● ● ●

I can't stand Russian nesting dolls.
They're so full of themselves.

Everything Bagels
● ● ●

Just between you and me, I think
"everything" bagels are making a lot of
promises they can't keep.

Friendly Competition...
● ● ●

My girlfriend and I often laugh about how
competitive we are. But I laugh more.

Getting Sick
● ● ●

How do you prevent a summer cold—
catch it in the winter!

Happiness

• • •

Some cause happiness wherever they go.
Others whenever they go.

I Always Wanted to Be Somebody

• • •

I always wanted to be somebody,
but I guess I should've been more specific.

Scoring

• • •

If winning isn't everything, why do they
keep score?

Imagination

• • •

Some people hear voices.
Some see invisible people.
Others have no imagination whatsoever.

---------- ★ **ALEXA'S FAVORITE**

I Do
• • •

Our wedding was so beautiful,
even the cake was in tiers.

Voices
• • •

The voices in my head may not be real,
but they have some good ideas!

A Shark's Favorite Line
• • •

Man overboard!

Learning in Switzerland
• • •

My parents sent me to military
school in Switzerland.
There they taught me how to be neutral.

---------- ★ **ALEXA'S FAVORITE**

What's Your Beef?
• • •

Becoming a vegetarian is
a huge missed steak.

Meet and Greet
• • •

Spotted outside a church in Michigan:
"Honk if you love Jesus. Keep on texting
while you drive if you want to meet him."

Sure About That?
• • •

So what if I don't know what "Armageddon"
means? It's not the end of the world.

No!
• • •

Do you know this joke where all the idiots
say no? [NO]

Middle Name
• • •

The sole purpose of a your parents giving
you a middle name, is so you can tell
when your really in trouble.

Skydiving
• • •

You do not need a parachute to skydive.
You only need a parachute to skydive twice.

Problems
• • •

Laugh at your problems.
Everybody else does.

Dolphins
• • •

Did you know that dolphins are so smart
that within a few weeks of captivity, they
can train people to stand on the very edge
of the pool and throw them fish?

School
Silliness

School Daze

Locked Out

Q: Why was the music teacher not able to open his classroom?

A: Because his keys were on the piano.

Trainer

Q: What's the difference between a teacher and a steam train?

A: The first says "Spit out that chewing gum" and the second says "Chew chew."

Schooling

Q: What did you learn in school today?

A: Not enough. I have to go back tomorrow.

Handwriting

Q: Teacher: Why is your homework in your father's handwriting?

A: Student: I used his pen.

---------- ★ **ALEXA'S FAVORITE**

Giraffes in School

Q: Why don't you see giraffes in elementary school?

A: Because they're all in high school.

Teacher's Favorite

Q: What is a teacher's three favorite words?

A: June, July and August.

Pals

Q: Who is your best friend at school?

A: Your princi-PAL.

School Bus

Q: What would happen if you took the school bus home?

A: The police would make you bring it back!

---------- ★ ALEXA'S FAVORITE

Report Card

Q: Why was the student's report card wet?

A: Because it was below C level.

- -

Flowers

Q: What's the best place to grow flowers in school?

A: In kindergarden.

Witch Class

Q: What school subject is a witch good at?

A: Spelling.

Food for Thought

Q: What vegetables do librarians like?

A: Quiet peas.

Brilliant

Q:Why did the teacher wear sunglasses?

A: Because his students were so bright!

Sky School

Q: Why did the students study in the airplane?

A: Because they wanted higher grades.

Teacher's Favorite

Q: What's a teacher's favorite nation?

A: Explanation.

Geography

Earthquake

Q: What did the ground say to the earthquake?

A: You crack me up.

Big Cow

Q: Which is the biggest cow in the world that doesn't give milk?

A: Moscow.

Overcrowded Tower

Q: Which tower couldn't fit any more people inside?

A: The I Full Tower.

Cold Country

Q: What is the coldest country in the world?

A: Chile.

Dead Sea

Q: Teacher: What can you tell me about the Dead Sea?

A: Student: I didn't even know it was sick!

---------- ★ ALEXA'S FAVORITE

Unusual River

Q: Why is Mississippi such an unusual river?

A: It has four eyes but it still can't see anything.

Alaska

Q: What is the capital of Alaska?

A: Come on, Juneau this one!

---------- ★ **ALEXA'S FAVORITE**

Penguin Fear

Q: Why don't you see penguins in Great Britain?

A: Because they're afraid of Wales.

Fast Country

Q: What is the fastest country in the world?

A: Rush-a!

India

Q: What's in the middle of India?

A: The letter D.

O!

Q: What is round at each end and high in the middle?

A: Ohio.

Dry Water

Q: Where do you find oceans without water?

A: On a map.

Capital

Q: What is the capital of Washington?

A: The W!

Rocking Men

Q: What rock group has four men that don't sing?

A: Mount Rushmore!

---------- ★ **ALEXA'S FAVORITE**

Astute State

Q: What is the smartest state?

A: Alabama—it has four A's and one B.

Math

4/1 Eyes

Q: Why should you wear glasses during math class?

A: They say it improves division.

An Odd Joke

Q: Why do teenagers always travel in groups of 3, 5, or 7?

A: Because they can't even.

Book Problems

Q: What did one math book say to the other?

A: Don't bother me, I've got my own problems!

-----------★ **ALEXA'S FAVORITE**

New Angles

Q: How do you stay warm in an empty room?

A: Go stand in the corner—it's always 90 degrees.

Number's Lunch

Q: Why did the two 4's skip lunch?

A: They already 8 (ate)!

Monster Math

Q: Are monsters good at math?

A: No, unless you Count Dracula.

Shapeless

Q: What did the triangle say to the circle?

A: You're pointless.

Favorite Sum...

Q: What is a math teacher's favorite sum?

A: Summer.

Mermaidematics

Q: What did the mermaid wear to math class?

A: An algae-bra.

--------- ★ ALEXA'S FAVORITE

Out of Shape

Q: What is the hardest shape to get out of?

A: The trap-azoid.

----

2 Fast

Q: What did 2 say to 4 after 2 beat him in a race?

A: 2 Fast 4U!

Square Shape

Q: What did the circle say to the rectangle?

A: You're such a square.

Drowned in Data

Q: Did you hear about the statistician who drowned crossing a river?

A: It was 3 feet deep, on average.

Middle School Math

Q: What do you get if you add two apples and three apples?

A: A middle school math problem!

No Tables

Q: The teacher asked Jack, why are you doing your multiplication on the floor?

A: Jack replied: You told me not to use tables.

History

Life Before Birth

Q: Why aren't you doing well in history?

A: Because the teacher keeps on asking about things that happened before I was born!

Ancient Greece

Q: What was the most popular story in Ancient Greece?

A: Troy Story.

George Washington

Q: Why did George Washington chop down the cherry tree?

A: No reason—he was stumped.

Egyptian

Q: Why was the Egyptian girl worried?

A: Because her daddy was a mummy.

- - - - - - - - - ★ **ALEXA'S FAVORITE**

Dark Ages

Q: Why were the early days of history called the Dark Ages?

A: Because there were so many knights.

- -

Independence

Q: Where was the Declaration of Independence signed?

A: At the bottom.

Lighting the Ark

Q: What kind of lighting did Noah use for the ark?

A: Floodlights!

Landing

Q: Where did the pilgrims land when they came to America?

A: On their feet.

---------- ★ ALEXA'S FAVORITE

History

Q: What is the fruitiest subject at school?

A: History, because it's full of dates!

Clean Up

Q: Who cleaned up after the animals on the ark?

A: I have Noah idea!

Parking Lots

Q: Where did the medieval knights park their camels?

A: Camelot.

Science

Angry Astronaut

Q: What do astronauts do when they get angry?

A: Blast off!

Shocking Discovery

Q: How did Ben Franklin feel after discovering electricity?

A: Shocked!

- - - - - - - - - - ★ ALEXA'S FAVORITE

Weather or Not, Here I Come

Q: What is a tornado's favorite game to play?

A: Twister!

- -

Dinnertime

Q: How do astronauts serve dinner?

A: On flying saucers.

He Has a Point

Q: What would you call a funny element?

A: He He He (helium helium helium).

We Never Want This Rain To Go Away

Q: What do clouds do when they become rich?

A: They make it rain!

--------- ★ ALEXA'S FAVORITE

Sun Smarts

Q: Why didn't the sun go to college?

A: Because it already had a million degrees!

Floating Away

Q: Did you hear about the chemist who was reading a book about helium?

A: Yup, he couldn't put it down!

Ice, Ice Baby

Q: If H_2O is the formula for water, what is the formula for ice?

A: H_2O cubed.

Doorbell

Q: Why did the scientist take out his doorbell?

A: He wanted to win the No-bell prize!

It's All Relative

Q: What did people say when Albert Einstein published a theory about space in 1905?

A: It was about time.

Lunch Time

Q: When do astronauts eat their lunch?

A: At launch time.

Saturn

Q: How do you know Saturn was married more than once?

A: Because she has a lot of rings.

Period Pun

Q: Why do people make bad chemistry jokes?

A: Because all the good ones argon.

Answer Me!

Q: Why are chemists great for solving problems?

A: They have all the solutions.

Reading

Q: What do planets like to read?

A: Comet books!

- - - - - - - - - ★ **ALEXA'S FAVORITE**

Minty Fresh

Q: What do scientists use to freshen their breath?

A: Experi-mints!

- -

Sliding

Q: Why did the germ cross the microscope?

A: To get to the other slide!

He Was Spacing Out

Q: Did you hear the one about the astronaut who stepped in gum?

A: He got stuck in Orbit.

Amusing
Animals

Beary Funny

Q: What did the sleepy Australian bear say at the job interview?

A: "I believe I am koala-fied for this position."

Self-Centered Oysters

Q: How come oysters never donate to charity?

A: Because they are shellfish.

--------- ★ ALEXA'S FAVORITE

Animals with Smarts

Q: What's the smartest animal?

A: A fish because they stay in schools!

Money Stinks

Q: How much money does a skunk have?

A: One scent!

Pain in the Tail

Q: What would a cat say if you stepped on its tail?

A: "Me-OW!"

Shark Bite

Q: What does a shark and a computer have in common?

A: They both have megabites.

Two Giraffes Are Driving...

Q: What do you get when two giraffes collide?

A: A giraffic jam.

Fishy Thoughts

Q: How do fish end their work emails?

A: Let minnow what you think.

Big Ant

Q: What kind of ant is even bigger than an elephant?

A: A gi-ant.

Dinosaur

Q: What do you call a sleeping dinosaur?

A: A dino-snore!

Caller I.D.

Q: What does my dog and my phone have in common?

A: They both have collar I.D.

Bug Plus Bird

Q: What do you get when you cross a centipede with a parrot?

A: A walkie-talkie!

Horse Down

Q: What did the horse say when it fell?

A: I've fallen and I can't giddyup!

- - - - - - - - - ★ **ALEXA'S FAVORITE**

Dog Breeds

Q: Which dog breed is guaranteed to laugh at all of your jokes?

A: A Chi-ha-ha!

- -

Seal Jokes

Q: What did the seal say when his friend told him a joke?

A: That's the sealiest thing I've ever heard!

Dog School

Q: What do dogs do after they finish obedience school?

A: They get their masters.

- - - - - - - - - - ★ **ALEXA'S FAVORITE**

Frogmobile

Q: What happened when the frog's car broke down on the side of the road?

A: It got toad away.

- -

Abra Cadabra!

Q: What do you call a dog magician?

A: A labracadabrador.

Bones Bones Bones

Q: What did the skeleton say to the puppy?

A: Bonappetite.

Lion

Q: What time is it when a lion walks into the room?

A: Time to get out of the room.

Giraffe Amends

Q: Why are giraffes so slow to apologize?

A: It takes them a long time to swallow their pride.

Elephant Trunks

Q: Why did the elephants get kicked out of the public pool?

A: They kept dropping their trunks.

Marine Dog

Q: How are a dog and a marine biologist alike?

A: One wags a tail and the other tags a whale.

Neighbor

Q: What do you call a horse that lives next door?

A: A neigh-bor!

Duck Shot

Q: Why was the duck put into the basketball game?

A: To make a fowl shot!

Clown Food

Q: Why did the lion spit out the clown?

A: Because he tasted funny.

Off to College

Q: What did the buffalo say to his son when he went off to college?

A: Bison.

Hot Dog!

Q: What do you give a dog with a fever?

A: Mustard, its the best thing for a hot dog!

Squash

Q: What game does the brontosaurus like to play with humans?

A: Squash.

Pisces Plus Mammal

Q: What do you get when you cross a fish with an elephant?

A: Swimming trunks!

Bad Kitty

Q: What's the worst kind of cat?

A: A cat-astrophe.

---------- ★ **ALEXA'S FAVORITE**

Moovies

Q: Why did the cow cross the road?

A: To get to the mooovie theater!

Frog Delight

Q: Why was the frog happy?

A: Because he ate everything that bugged him!

Purrrfect Strike

Q: What do you call a cat that goes bowling?

A: An alley cat.

Shellfish Loans

Q: Where do shellfish go to borrow money?

A: The prawn broker.

This Little Dog Went to the Market

Q: What type of market should you NEVER take your dog?

A: A flea market!

Serpents Plus Sweets

Q: What do you get when you cross a snake with a tasty dessert?

A: A pie-thon!

Dirty Dog

Q: What do you call a black Eskimo dog?

A: A dusky husky!

Bear Shoes

Q: Why don't bears wear shoes?

A: They'd still have bear feet!

Perfect
Puns

Space Party

Q: How do you organize a space party?

A: You planet.

2:30 Dentist

Q: What's the best time to go to the dentist?

A: Tooth hurty.

Culturally Significant

Q: Why does yogurt love going to museums?

A: Because it's cultured.

Swimming

Q: Is this pool safe for diving?

A: It deep ends.

---------- ★ **ALEXA'S FAVORITE**

Baby

Q: How do you put a baby alien to sleep?

A: You rocket.

King's Rain

Q: What is a king's favorite kind of precipitation?

A: Hail!

Population Pun

Q: Which country's capital has the fastest-growing population?

A: Ireland. Every day it's Dublin.

Hi Ya!

Q: What do you call a pig that does karate?

A: Pork chop.

Sad Magician

Q: Why did the magician have to cancel his show?

A: He'd just washed his hare and couldn't do a thing with it.

Beaten-up Dino

Q: What do you call a T-Rex that's been beaten up?

A: Dino-sore.

Award-winning

Q: Why did the scarecrow win an award?

A: Because he was outstanding in his field.

Rude Reindeer

Q: What do you call an obnoxious reindeer?

A: RUDEolph.

Maybee I Will, Maybee I Won't

Q: What do you call a bee that can't make up its mind?

A: Maybee.

Trees of Christmas Past

Q: Why are Christmas trees so fond of the past?

A: Because the present's beneath them.

Behind Bars

Q: If prisoners could take their own mugshots, what would they be called?

A: CELLphies.

Chemist Dogs

Q: What do chemists' dogs do with their bones?

A: They barium!

How Sweet

Q: Why do watermelons have fancy weddings?

A: Because they cantaloupe.

Class with Claus

Q: What do you say to Santa when he's taking attendance at school?

A: Present.

Doctor at Sea

Q: What did sick people do on the Mayflower?

A: They went to the dock!

Always in the Shop

Q: Why did the butcher work extra hours at the shop?

A: To make ends meat.

Dough for the Poor

Q: Why did the poor man sell yeast?

A: To raise some dough.

---------- ★ **ALEXA'S FAVORITE**

Beat in Battle

Q: Why was King Arthur's army too tired to fight?

A: It had too many sleepless knights.

- -

Foggy La

Q: What happens when fog lifts in California?

A: UCLA!

An Icy Ride

Q: How does a snowman get to work?

A: By icicle.

Hilarious
Holidays

Valentine's

A Big Dill

Q: What did the pickle say to the other pickle on Valentine's Day?

A: "You mean a great dill to me."

Caught the Love Bug

Q: Did you hear about the bed bugs who fell in love?

A: They're getting married in the spring!

Cannoli Gift

Q: Why did Sam give his girlfriend a cannoli for Valentine's Day?

A: Because he "cannoli" be happy when he is with her.

Made Just for You

Q: What Valentine's Day candy is best to give a girl?

A: Her-She Kisses.

---------- ★ **ALEXA'S FAVORITE**

Broken Heart

Q: What did the guy with the broken leg say to his nurse?

A: "I've got a crutch on you."

- -

Pencil and Paper

Q: What did the pencil say to the paper?

A: "I dot my I's on you!"

Small Packages

Q: What do you call a very small valentine?

A: A valen-tiny!

Electricity

Q: What did the lightbulb say to the other lightbulb on Valentine's Day?

A: "I love you a watt."

Slithering Romance

Q: What did one snake say to the other snake?

A: "Give me a little hug and a hiss, honey."

Gardener in Love

Q: What happened when the man fell in love with his garden?

A: It made him wed his plants!

School Supplies Love

Q: What did the calculator say to the pencil on Valentine's Day?

A: "You can always count on me."

Mushroom Love

Q: What did one mushroom say to the other on Valentine's Day?

A: "There's so mushroom in my heart for you!"

Owl Love

Q: What did the boy owl say to the girl owl on Valentine's Day?

A: "Owl be yours!"

Valentine's Day Envelope

Q: What did the Valentine's Day card say to the stamp?

A: "Stick with me and you'll go places."

Thermometer Love

Q: What did the thermometer say to the other thermometer?

A: "You make my temperature rise."

Man Overboard

Q: What is the difference between a girl who is sick of her boyfriend and a sailor who falls into the ocean?

A: One is bored over a man; the other is a man overboard.

- -

A Ton of Love

Q: What did the elephant say to his girlfriend?

A: "I love you a ton!"

Runaway Bride

Q: If your aunt ran off to get married on Valentine's, what would you call her?

A: Antelope.

Easter

I See You

Q: Why does the Easter bunny hide?

A: Because he's a little chicken.

Runny Egg

Q: What sport are the eggs good at?

A: Running.

Jewelry

Q: What kind of jewelry do rabbits wear?

A: 14 carrot gold.

---------- ★ ALEXA'S FAVORITE

Easter Bunny Jams

Q: What music does the Easter bunny like?

A: Hip-hop.

- -

Can I See Your License?

Q: Why does Peter Cottontail go hopping down the bunny trail?

A: Because he's too young to drive.

That's Egg-cellent!

Q: Why is it forbidden to tell a joke to your Easter eggs?

A: You wouldn't want to crack them up.

Carrot Snacks

Q: What did the Easter bunny say to the carrot?

A: "It's been nice gnawing you."

Yuck It Up

Q: What did one Easter egg say to the other?

A: "Heard any good yolks today?"

Therapy

Q: Therapist to chocolate bunny: "What's been up lately?"

A: Chocolate bunny: "I don't know, Doc, I just feel so hollow inside."

Sparks Are Flying

Q: What did the flame say to his buddies after he fell in love?

A: "I found the perfect match!"

Egg Day

Q: What day does an Easter egg hate the most?

A: Fry-day

Shiny Nose

Q: Why does the Easter bunny have a shiny nose?

A: His powder puff is on the wrong end.

Easter Bunny Exercise

Q: How does the Easter bunny stay fit?

A: Eggs-ercise.

---------- ★ **ALEXA'S FAVORITE**

Ski Bunny

Q: Where did the Easter Bunny learn how to ski?

A: The bunny hill.

What's Up, Doc?

Q: What do you call a rabbit that can tell a good joke?

A: A funny bunny.

Rabbit Hole

Q: What do you get if you pour hot water down a rabbit hole?

A: Hot cross bunnies!

Easter Eggs

Q: Where does the Easter bunny
   get his eggs?

A: From eggplant.

Misbehaved Bunny

Q: What happened to the Easter bunny
   at school?

A: He was eggspelled.

Luck of the Bunny

Q: Why is a bunny the luckiest animal in
   the world?

A: It has four rabbits' feet.

Bunny Dance

Q: Where do Easter bunnies dance?

A: At the basket-ball.

Halloween

Halloween Recess

Q: What is a recess at a mortuary called?

A: A coffin break!

Sickly Vampire

Q: How can you tell if a vampire has a horrible cold?

A: By his deep loud coffin!

Dancing Monsters

Q: What kind of monster loves to disco?

A: The boogieman.

Ahoy, Dracula!

Q: How do vampires get around on Halloween?

A: On blood vessels.

Vampire Love

Q: What's it like to be kissed by a vampire?

A: It's a pain in the neck.

Lumberjacks

Q: Why are skeletons so good at chopping down trees?

A: They're LUMBAR-jacks!

A Vampire's Nightcap

Q: What did one thirsty vampire say to the other as they were passing the morgue?

A: Let's stop in for a cool one!

- - - - - - - - - - ★ **ALEXA'S FAVORITE**

Ghost on R&R

Q: Where does a ghost go on vacation?

A: Mali-boo.

Dieting Scarecrow

Q: Why didn't the scarecrow eat dinner?

A: He was already stuffed.

Angry Vampire

Q: What is a vampire's pet peeve?

A: A tourniquet!

Ghost Makeup

Q: What do female ghosts use to do their makeup?

A: Vanishing cream!

---------- ★ ALEXA'S FAVORITE

Obese Pumpkin

Q: What do you call a fat pumpkin?

A: A plumpkin.

- -

Intellectual Vampire

Q: Why did the vampire read the
   New York Times?

A: He heard it had great circulation.

Doctor's Orders

Q: Did you hear about the skeleton that
   dropped out of medical school?

A: He just didn't have the stomach for it.

Pumpkin Pedestrians

Q: Who helps little pumpkins cross the road
   on the way to school?

A: The crossing gourd!

Skeleton Dance Dilemma

Q: Why didn't the skeleton dance at the
   Halloween party?

A: He had no body to dance with!

Workaholic Horseman

Q: Why did the headless horseman go into business?

A: He wanted to get ahead in life.

---------- ★ ALEXA'S FAVORITE

Panda Ghost

Q: What does a panda ghost eat?

A: Bam-BOO!

Congested Ghost

Q: What is in a ghost's nose?

A: Boo-gers.

Potluck BBQ

Q: What did the skeleton bring to the picnic?

A: His appetite and lots of spare ribs!

Thanksgiving

Thanksgiving and Halloween

Q: What do Thanksgiving and Halloween have in common?

A: One has gobblers, the other goblins.

New Neighbors

Q: What did one turkey say to the other when they saw the Pilgrims land at Plymouth rock?

A: "They look nice. Maybe they'll have us over for dinner."

---------- ★ ALEXA'S FAVORITE

Turkey Legs

Q: Where do you find a turkey with no legs?

A: Exactly where you left it...

Turkey Search Engine

Q: What did the turkey say to the computer?

A: "Google, google, google!"

Barn Roof

Q: What do you get when a turkey lays an egg on a barn roof?

A: An eggroll.

---------- ★ ALEXA'S FAVORITE

Turkey Jump

Q: Can a turkey jump higher than the Empire State Building?

A: Of course—buildings can't jump at all.

Turkey on the Job

Q: Why did the turkey cross the road?

A: It was the chicken's day off!

Turkey Instrument

Q: Why did the turkey play the drums in his band?

A: Because he already had drumsticks!

Where does a Turkey Come From?

Q: Fruit comes from a fruit tree, so where does turkey come from?

A: A poul-tree.

Full Turkey

Q: What did the turkey say before it was roasted?

A: "Boy, I'm stuffed!"

Turkeys and Football

Q: What is it called when a turkey fumbles in football?

A: A fowl play.

Turkey Feathers

Q: Which side of the turkey has the most feathers?

A: The outside!

Turkey Toys

Q: What was the turkey looking for at Toys R Us?

A: Gobbleheads.

Turkey Hunt

Q: What did the turkey say to the turkey hunter?

A: "Quack, quack, quack."

Turkey with a Broken Leg

Q: What sound does a limping turkey make?

A: Wobble, wobble!

---------- ★ **ALEXA'S FAVORITE**

Thankful for Being Human

Q: When asked to write a composition entitled, "What I'm thankful for on Thanksgiving," what did little Johnny write?

A: "I am thankful that I'm not a turkey."

Extra Stuffing

Q: Why did the turkey refuse dessert?

A: He was stuffed.

Mother Turkey

Q: Why did the turkey sit on the tomahawk?

A: To hatchet.

Red Cranberries

Q: Why did the cranberries turn red?

A: Because they saw the turkey dressing!

Christmas

Gingerbread Man

Q: Why was the gingerbread man robbed?

A: A: Because of his dough.

Kids Say the Darnedest Things

Q: Why did the children call St. Nick "Santa Caus"?

A: Because there was Noël.

---------- ★ ALEXA'S FAVORITE

iPad

Q: What do you get when you combine a Christmas tree with an iPad?

A: A pineapple.

Santa Hits the Shore

Q: When Santa is on the beach, what do the elves call him?

A: Sandy Claus.

Dunk!

Q: Why did the basketball player love gingerbread cookies so much?

A: He loved to dunk them.

Elf Therapy

Q: Why was Santa's little helper feeling depressed?

A: Because he had low elf esteem.

Santa the Sleuth

Q: What do you get if you cross Father Christmas with a detective?

A: Santa Clues!

Open Mic Night at the North Pole

Q: What did the reindeer say before telling his joke?

A: This one'll sleigh you!

Jingle, Rinse, and Spin

Q: What is Santa Claus' laundry detergent of choice?

A: Yule-Tide.

---------- ★ **ALEXA'S FAVORITE**

Double Parked

Q: Why did Santa get a parking ticket last Christmas Eve?

A: He was making a special delivery and left his sleigh in a snow parking zone.

Now I Know My ABCs

Q: How does Santa sing the alphabet?

A: A B C D E F G... H I J K L M N Oh!, Oh!, Oh!, P Q R S T U V W X Y Z!

Breakfast

Q: What do snowmen eat for breakfast?

A: Frosted Flakes.

Maybe Even a Standing O-Ho-Ho

Q: What do the elves call it when Father Christmas claps his hands at the end of a play?

A: Santapplause!

Lost Tail

Q: What would a reindeer do if it lost its tail?

A: He'd go to a "re-tail" shop for a new one!

Sleigh Ride Through the Rain

Q: How can Santa deliver presents during a thunderstorm?

A: His sleigh is flown by raindeer.

Claus' Canine

Q: What's Santa's dog's name?

A: Santa Paws!

Pringle Bells

Q: What's Santa Claus' favorite type of potato chip?

A: Crisp Pringles!

Sporty Santa

Q: What's Santa Claus' favorite track and field event?

A: North Pole-vaulting!

That's Gonna Leave a Mark

Q: What do you get if Santa goes down the chimney when a fire is lit?

A: Crisp Kringle.

---------- ★ ALEXA'S FAVORITE

Jacket Snaps

Q: How do gingerbread men keep their jackets closed?

A: With ginger snaps.

- -

Body Double

Q: What's as big as Santa but weighs nothing?

A: Santa's shadow!

When the Sleigh's in the Shop

Q: What kind of bike does Santa Claus ride?

A: A Holly Davidson.

Also Available from Reader's Digest

Laughter, the Best Medicine

More than 600 jokes, gags, and laugh lines. Drawn from one of the most popular features of *Reader's Digest* magazine, this lighthearted collection of jokes, one-liners, and other glimpses of life is just what the doctor ordered.

ISBN 978-0-89577-977-9 • $9.95 paperback

Laughter Still Is the Best Medicine

This hilarious collection offers up some of the funniest moments that get us through our day, with jokes, gags, and cartoons that will have readers laughing out loud.

ISBN 978-1-62145-137-2 • $9.95 paperback

Laughter Totally Is the Best Medicine

More than 1,000 of the funniest, laugh-out-loud jokes, quips, quotes, anecdotes, and cartoons from *Reader's Digest* magazine—guaranteed to put laughter in your day.

ISBN 978-1-62145-406-9 • $9.99 paperback

3 1333 04894 4860

Fun Jokes For Funny Kids

Loaded with knock-knock jokes, riddles, one-liners, tongue twisters, and puns, *Fun Jokes for Funny Kids* will keep kids ages 6 to 12 rolling in laughter.

ISBN 978-1-62145-438-0 • $6.99 paperback

For more information, visit us at RDTradePublishing.com.
E-book editions are also available.

Reader's Digest books can be purchased through
retail and online bookstores.